Mind Your Mind Space

Your Comprehensive Guide to Achieving
Mental Wellness and Resilience

MIND YOUR MIND SPACE

Your Comprehensive Guide to Achieving Mental Wellness and Resilience

Mindful Maven

Disclaimer

The information contained in this book is intended for general informational and educational purposes only. It is not intended to be a substitute for professional medical advice, diagnosis, or treatment. Always seek the advice of a qualified healthcare provider with any questions you may have regarding a medical condition or treatment.

The author and publisher of this book make no representations or warranties of any kind, express or implied, about the completeness, accuracy, reliability, suitability, or availability with respect to the content of this book or the information, products, services, or related graphics contained in this book for any purpose. Any reliance you place on such information is therefore strictly at your own risk.

In no event will the author or publisher be liable for any loss or damage including without limitation, indirect or consequential loss or damage, or any loss or damage whatsoever arising from loss of data or profits arising out of, or in connection with, the use of this book.

Every effort has been made to ensure that the information in this book is accurate and up-to-date at the time of publication. However, the author and publisher do not guarantee or warrant the accuracy, completeness, or usefulness of any information or advice contained in this book.

Table of Contents

<u>affects them</u>

Chapter 3: The Power of Positive Thinking

- <u>Examining the benefits of positive thinking for mental health, such as reduced stress and improved self-esteem</u>

- <u>Providing practical tips for cultivating a more positive mindset, such as gratitude exercises and reframing negative thoughts</u>

Chapter 4: Managing Stress and Anxiety

- <u>The danger Stress and Anxiety pose to Mental Health</u>

- <u>Strategies for managing stress and anxiety, such as mindfulness, relaxation techniques, and self-care practices</u>

Chapter 5: Cultivating Resilience

- <u>Exploring the concept of resilience and how it can help us bounce back from adversity</u>

- <u>Discussing the traits of resilient individuals</u>

- <u>How to develop these traits in ourselves</u>

Chapter 6: Building Strong Relationships

- Examining the impact of social support on mental health

- Providing strategies for building and maintaining strong relationships, such as effective communication and boundary-setting

Chapter 7: Mindfulness and Self-Awareness

- Discussing the benefits of mindfulness and self-awareness for mental health

- Providing exercises and practices for cultivating mindfulness and self-awareness

Chapter 8: The Role of Physical Health

- The relationship between physical health and mental health will be examined.

- Providing strategies for improving physical health, such as exercise and healthy eating, and discussing how these strategies can improve mental health as well

- Dietary timetable that is essential for the

<u>development of our mental health</u>

<u>Chapter 9: Overcoming Mental Health Challenges</u>

- <u>Discussing common mental health challenges, such as depression and anxiety, and how to overcome them</u>

- <u>Providing resources and support for readers who are struggling with mental health issues</u>

<u>Chapter 10: Maintaining a Healthy Mind Space</u>

- <u>The importance of self-care, stress management, and finding balance in our lives</u>

- <u>Providing practical tips for maintaining a healthy mind space over the long term</u>

- <u>Summarizing the key takeaways from the book</u>

Preface

Welcome to Mind Your Mind Space, a comprehensive guide to improving your mental health and well-being. In today's fast-paced world, it's more important than ever to prioritize our mental health and take steps to maintain a healthy mind space. This book will provide you with practical tips, strategies, and resources for improving your mental health and living a more balanced life.

Throughout this book, we'll explore various aspects of mental health, including the impact of stress and anxiety, the importance of resilience, building strong relationships, mindfulness and self-awareness, physical health, overcoming mental health challenges, and maintaining a healthy mind space. We'll provide you with evidence-based strategies and techniques that you can use to improve your mental health, as well as resources for seeking professional help if needed.

Whether you're struggling with mental health issues, looking to prevent burnout, or simply want to maintain a healthy mind space, this book is for you. We believe that by taking care of our mental health, we can live happier, more fulfilling lives. So, let's dive in and start taking steps towards a healthier mind space.

Chapter 1

Mind Your Mind Space

Mind Your Mind Space

Mental health is a vital aspect of our overall well-being. It affects how we think, feel, and act, and it plays a crucial role in our ability to lead fulfilling lives. However, many people struggle with maintaining good mental health, which can lead to a range of problems, including depression, anxiety, and other mental health disorders.

In recent years, there has been a growing interest in the concept of "mind space" and how it can impact our mental health. Mind space refers to the mental landscape that we inhabit, which includes our thoughts, emotions, beliefs, and attitudes. It is the lens through which we view the world, and it shapes our experiences and interactions with others.

The idea that we can actively shape our mind space to improve our mental health is an empowering one. It means that we have the power to take control of our mental health and make positive changes that can have a significant impact on our lives.

This book is designed to help readers understand their mind space and learn strategies for improving their mental health. We will explore the different components of mind space and how they interact with each other to impact our mental health. We will also provide practical tips and exercises for cultivating a positive mindset, managing stress and anxiety, building resilience, cultivating strong relationships, and improving physical health.

By the end of this book, readers will have a better understanding of their mind space and the role it plays in their mental health. They will also have practical strategies and tools for improving their mental health and maintaining a healthy mind space over the long term.

Defining the Concept of Mind Space

Mind space is a term used to describe the mental landscape that we inhabit. It includes our thoughts, emotions, beliefs, attitudes, and perceptions, all of which shape how we experience the world around us.

Our mind space is like a lens through which we view the world. It affects how we interpret and respond to events, people, and situations, and it plays a crucial role in our mental health and overall well-being. It is not a physical place, but rather a metaphorical space that exists within our minds.

The concept of mind space is based on the idea that our thoughts and emotions are not passive experiences that happen to us, but rather active processes that we can shape and influence. By understanding our mind space, we can become more aware of the thoughts and emotions that impact our mental health and take steps to improve it.

The components of mind space are interconnected and can influence each other. For example, our beliefs and attitudes can shape our thoughts, which in turn can impact our emotions and behaviors. Similarly, our emotions can influence our thoughts and beliefs, creating a feedback loop that can either support or undermine our mental health.

By becoming more aware of our mind space and the way it shapes our experiences, we can take steps to cultivate a more positive and supportive mental landscape. This can involve strategies like positive thinking, mindfulness, self-awareness, and building strong relationships.

Overall, the concept of mind space highlights the importance of paying attention to our thoughts, emotions, beliefs, and attitudes, and understanding how they interact with each other to impact our mental health. By actively shaping our mind space, we can improve our mental health and lead more fulfilling lives.

Discussing the Importance of Mental Health and How it Affects Our Overall Well-Being

Mental health is an essential component of our overall well-being. It refers to our emotional, psychological, and social well-being and influences how we think, feel, and behave in our daily lives.

Good mental health allows us to cope with the challenges we face, build positive relationships, and lead fulfilling lives.

Mental health affects every aspect of our lives, including our physical health, relationships, work, and personal growth. When we have good mental health, we are better able to manage stress, cope with difficult situations, and make healthy choices that support our physical health.

Conversely, poor mental health can have a significant negative impact on our overall well-being. It can lead to physical health problems such as headaches, digestive issues, and chronic pain, as well as difficulties in relationships and work. It can also lead to substance abuse, self-harm, and suicide, making it a critical issue to address.

Despite the importance of mental health, it is often overlooked or stigmatized in society. Many people still view mental health as a weakness or a personal failing, which can prevent individuals from seeking help when they need it.

It is essential to recognize that mental health is a fundamental aspect of our overall health, and seeking help when we are struggling is a sign of strength, not weakness. There are a variety of resources available, including therapy, support groups, and self-care practices, that can help us improve our mental health and lead fulfilling lives.

By prioritizing our mental health, we can improve our overall well-being, enhance our relationships, and increase our resilience in the face of life's challenges. It is never too late to start prioritizing mental health, and small steps can make a significant difference.

Introducing the Idea that We Can Actively Shape Our Mind Space to Improve Our Mental Health

While mental health is undoubtedly an important aspect of our overall well-being, it is often seen as something that is beyond our control. Many people believe that their thoughts and emotions are fixed and cannot be changed, which can lead to a sense of helplessness and despair when facing mental health challenges.

However, the reality is that we can actively shape

our mind space to improve our mental health. Mind space refers to the collection of thoughts, emotions, beliefs, and attitudes that make up our internal experience. Our perspective of the world and how we understand our experiences are shaped by the mind space.

By understanding and becoming aware of our mind space, we can begin to identify patterns of thought and behavior that may be contributing to our mental health challenges. We can then use various techniques to modify these patterns and develop healthier ways of thinking and behaving.

One technique that can be particularly effective in shaping our mind space is **cognitive-behavioral therapy (CBT)**. Cognitive behavioral therapy (CBT) is a form of therapy that involves talking and is centered on recognizing and modifying detrimental thought patterns and behaviors.. By working with a therapist, we can learn how to challenge negative thoughts and replace them with more positive and constructive ones.

Other techniques that can help shape our mind space include **mindfulness meditation**, which can help us become more aware of our thoughts and emotions and learn to observe them without judgment. **Gratitude exercises** can also be beneficial, as they help us shift our focus from negative to positive experiences and cultivate a more optimistic outlook.

It is important to remember that shaping our mind space is a process that takes time and effort. It requires a willingness to examine our thoughts and behaviors honestly and a commitment to making meaningful changes. However, the benefits of cultivating a healthy mind space are immeasurable and can lead to a more fulfilling and satisfying life.

Chapter 2

Understanding Your Mind Space

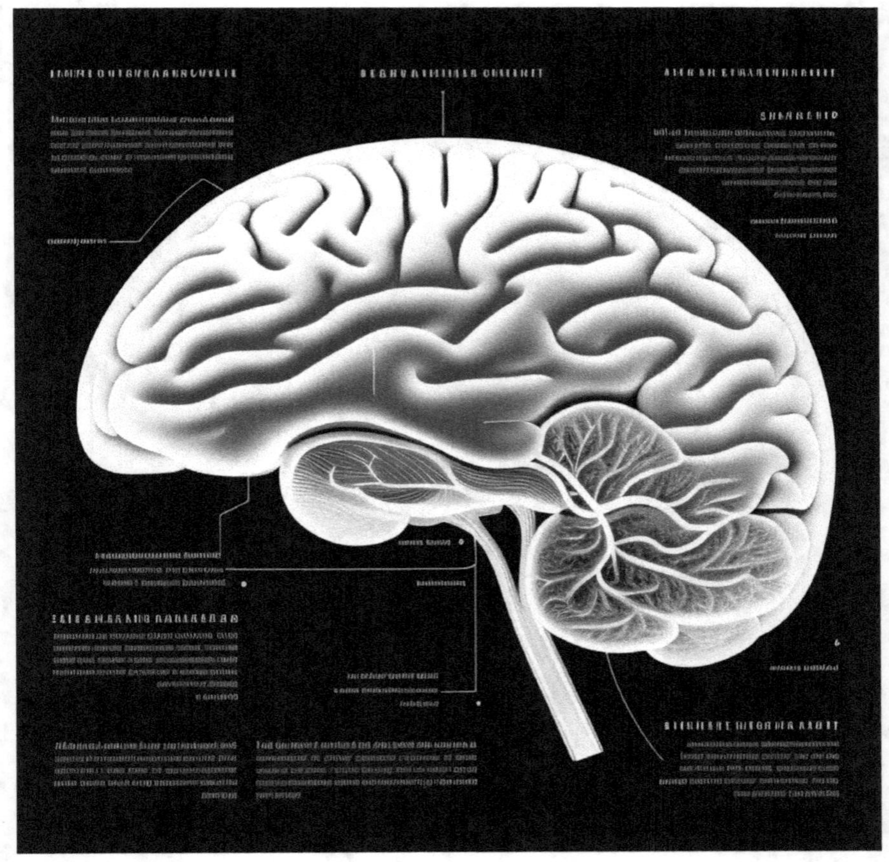

Understanding Your Mind Space

To actively shape our mind space to improve our mental health, it's important to first understand what our mind space is made up of. Our mind space is the collection of thoughts, emotions, beliefs, and attitudes that make up our internal experience. It acts as a filter through which we perceive the world and make sense of our encounters.

To gain a better understanding of our mind space, it can be helpful to break it down into its different components.

- **Thoughts**: Our thoughts are the ideas, opinions, and judgments that we have about ourselves, others, and the world around us. These thoughts and behaviors, whether positive or negative, have a significant impact on our emotions and actions.

- **Emotions**: Our emotions are the feelings that we experience in response to our thoughts and the events happening around us. Emotions can range from joy and happiness to anger and sadness, and can also have a significant impact on our behavior.

- **Beliefs**: Our beliefs are the assumptions and convictions we hold about ourselves, others, and the world around us. Our beliefs can be deeply ingrained and can influence how we interpret and respond to different situations.

- **Attitudes**: Our attitudes are the general outlooks or dispositions that we have towards certain things or people. Attitudes can be positive or negative and can impact how we interact with others and navigate the world around us.

These components of our mind space are not separate from one another, but rather interact with and influence each other. For example, our beliefs can shape our thoughts and attitudes, which in turn affect our emotions and behavior.

By becoming more aware of the components of our mind space, we can begin to identify patterns of thought and behavior that may be contributing to our mental health challenges. We can then work on modifying these patterns and developing healthier ways of thinking and behaving.

To gain a better understanding of our mind space, we can try journaling or speaking with a therapist. By examining our thoughts and feelings and discussing them with a professional, we can gain new insights into our mind space and begin to shape it in a more positive and healthy way.

Exploring the Different Components of Mind Space

The concept of mind space is made up of several different components that work together to influence our mental and emotional state. These components include thoughts, emotions, beliefs, and attitudes. In this section, we will explore each component in more detail.

- Thoughts: Our thoughts are the mental processes that involve perception, reasoning, and judgment. They can be positive or negative and can have a significant impact on our emotions and behavior. Our thoughts can be influenced by external factors, such as our environment or interactions with others, as well as internal factors, such as our beliefs and values.

- Emotions: Our emotions are our subjective experiences that are typically accompanied by physiological changes, such as changes in heart rate, breathing, and muscle tension. Emotions can be categorized as positive or negative and can range from joy and happiness to anger and sadness. They are often triggered by external or internal stimuli, such as a positive event or a negative memory.

- Beliefs: Our beliefs are the attitudes and convictions that we hold about ourselves, others, and the world around us. They can be positive or negative and can shape our thoughts, emotions, and behavior. Beliefs are often formed through our experiences and interactions with others, as well as through cultural and societal influences.

- Attitudes: Our attitudes are our overall dispositions or outlooks towards certain things or people. They can be positive or negative and can influence our behavior and interactions with others. Attitudes are often formed through our beliefs and experiences and can be changed through deliberate effort and exposure to new experiences.

It's important to note that these components are not separate from each other, but rather interact with and influence each other. For example, our beliefs can shape our thoughts and attitudes, which in turn affect our emotions and behavior.

By becoming more aware of these different components of our mind space, we can begin to identify patterns of thought and behavior that may be contributing to our mental health challenges. We can then work on modifying these patterns and developing healthier ways of thinking and behaving. This can lead to improved mental and emotional well-being and a more positive and fulfilling life.

How These Components Interact with Each Other and Impact Our Mental Health

The different components of mind space - thoughts, emotions, beliefs, and attitudes - are not isolated from each other. Instead, they interact with each other in complex ways, influencing our mental and emotional well-being.

For instance, our thoughts can influence our emotions, and vice versa. If we have negative thoughts, such as "I'm not good enough" or "I'm a failure," this can trigger negative emotions like sadness, anxiety, or self-doubt. Conversely, positive thoughts, such as "I can do this" or "I am worthy," can lead to positive emotions like happiness, confidence, or self-esteem.

Similarly, our beliefs can shape our attitudes, which can then influence our thoughts and emotions. For example, if we hold negative beliefs about ourselves, such as "I am unlovable" or "I am not smart enough," this can lead to negative attitudes towards ourselves and others, which in turn can lead to negative thoughts and emotions.

These components of mind space can also impact our behavior. Our attitudes, beliefs, thoughts, and emotions can shape our actions and reactions to situations. For instance, if we have a negative attitude towards a particular person or situation, we may act defensively or avoid it altogether. Alternatively, if we have a positive attitude towards something, we may approach it with enthusiasm and confidence.

It's important to recognize that these interactions can be both positive and negative. For example, positive thoughts and emotions can reinforce positive beliefs and attitudes, leading to a self-reinforcing cycle of positivity. On the other hand, negative thoughts and emotions can reinforce negative beliefs and attitudes, leading to a self-reinforcing cycle of negativity.

Ultimately, the way in which these components of mind space interact with each other can impact our mental and emotional well-being. If we can become more aware of these interactions and work to modify negative patterns of thought and behavior, we can improve our mental health and well-being. This may involve working on improving our self-talk, identifying and challenging negative beliefs, and developing more positive attitudes and outlooks towards ourselves and the world around us.

Providing Exercises to Help you Identify your Own Mind Space and Understand How It Affects you

To better understand and shape our mind space, it can be helpful to engage in exercises that help us identify our thoughts, emotions, beliefs, and attitudes, and how they interact with each other. Here are some exercises that can be useful:

- **Journaling**: Writing down our thoughts and feelings in a journal can help us identify patterns of thinking and feeling. We can reflect on our journal entries to gain insight into how our mind space is affecting our mental health and well-being.

- **Mindfulness meditation**: The practice of mindfulness meditation entails directing our attention to the current moment and acknowledging our thoughts and feelings without any evaluation or criticism. This can help us become more aware of our thought patterns and how they influence our emotions and behavior.

- **Self-reflection**: Taking time to reflect on our beliefs, values, and attitudes can help us identify any negative or limiting beliefs that may be holding us back. We can then work to challenge these beliefs and develop more positive and empowering ones.

- **Cognitive-behavioral therapy (CBT) exercises**: CBT is a type of therapy that focuses on identifying and changing negative thought patterns. CBT exercises, such as thought records, can help us identify and challenge negative thoughts that may be contributing to negative emotions and behaviors.

- **Gratitude practice**: Practicing gratitude involves intentionally focusing on the things in our lives that we are thankful for. This can help shift our focus from negative thoughts and emotions to positive ones, leading to improved mental health and well-being.

By engaging in these exercises, we can gain a better understanding of our mind space and how it is impacting our mental and emotional well-being. We can then work to modify any negative patterns of thought or behavior, and develop a more positive and empowering mind space.

Chapter 3

35

The Power of Positive Thinking

The Power of Positive Thinking

Having a positive mindset can greatly influence our mental health and general welfare. By concentrating on constructive thoughts, we can experience a greater sense of hopefulness, assurance, and drive, enabling us to deal with difficulties more optimistically and manage stress more efficiently.

A major advantage of positive thinking is that it can alleviate stress. When we focus on negative thoughts and worry, we can become overwhelmed and anxious, which can lead to increased stress levels. However, when we focus on positive thoughts, we can feel more relaxed and calm, which can help us to better manage stress.

Positive thinking can also improve our self-esteem. When we focus on positive aspects of ourselves and our lives, we can feel more confident and capable. This can help us to approach new challenges with a sense of self-assurance, rather than self-doubt.

Numerous methods exist to foster a positive outlook on life. A useful approach is to engage in gratitude exercises, which entails directing our attention to the beneficial aspects of our lives and expressing appreciation for them. One approach is to note down three things we are grateful for each day or acknowledge someone for their deeds. Additionally, we can restructure negative thoughts by transforming them into more positive ones.

This requires us to take a negative thought and discover a more constructive perspective to view the situation. For example, if we are feeling anxious about an upcoming presentation, we might reframe the thought from "I'm going to fail" to "I'm prepared and capable of doing my best."

Incorporating positive self-talk can also be helpful. This involves speaking to ourselves in a positive and encouraging way, rather than being self-critical. As an instance, rather than expressing "I am incapable of achieving this," we could express "I am capable of accomplishing this task, and I will put in my best effort." By fostering a more favorable attitude, we can enhance our psychological welfare and overall health. It takes practice and effort to develop a positive outlook, but the benefits are well worth it.

Examining the benefits of positive thinking for mental health, such as reduced stress and improved self-esteem

Research has demonstrated that adopting a positive mindset can have various advantages for psychological well-being, including the decrease of stress levels being one of the most significant benefits. When we approach situations with a positive mindset, we are better able to cope with stressors and are less likely to experience negative emotions such as anxiety and depression. This can also lead to better overall emotional regulation and a more positive outlook on life.

Additionally, positive thinking can improve self-esteem. When we focus on our strengths and accomplishments, we are more likely to feel good about ourselves and our abilities. This, in turn, can lead to increased confidence and motivation to pursue our goals.

Positive thinking has also been linked to better coping skills and resilience, which can help individuals better manage difficult situations and bounce back from adversity. This can lead to increased feelings of empowerment and a greater sense of control over one's life.

Research has also shown that positive thinking can improve physical health outcomes such as better cardiovascular health and a stronger immune system. This is likely because positive thinking is associated with lower levels of stress, which can have a negative impact on physical health.

Overall, incorporating positive thinking into our daily lives can have a profound impact on our mental and physical well-being. By focusing on the positive aspects of our lives and reframing negative thoughts, we can cultivate a more optimistic and fulfilling outlook on life.

Providing practical tips for cultivating a more positive mindset, such as gratitude exercises and reframing negative thoughts

Practical tips can be very helpful in cultivating a more positive mindset. Here are some effective tips that can help:

1. **Practice gratitude**: Establish a routine of jotting down three things that you appreciate each day. This helps to shift your focus from negative thoughts to positive ones.

2. **Reframe negative thoughts:** Whenever you have a negative thought, challenge it by asking yourself if it is really true. Attempt to reframe negative thoughts in a constructive manner, such as replacing "I'm not good enough" with "I am putting in my best effort." **Surround yourself with positivity**: Surround yourself with optimistic influences, like positive individuals, motivational phrases, and affirmations, to reinforce positive thinking.

3. **Visualize success**: Visualize success in your

endeavors to enhance your confidence and maintain your drive. Prioritize self-care by attending to your physical and emotional needs, such as getting enough rest, consuming nourishing foods, and engaging in regular physical activity to enhance your overall wellness and uplift your mood. Practice mindfulness by remaining present and attentive to the present moment.

4. **Practice self-care**: Prioritize self-care by attending to your physical and emotional needs, such as getting enough rest, consuming nourishing foods, and engaging in regular physical activity to enhance your overall wellness and uplift your mood. Practice mindfulness by remaining present and attentive to the present moment.

5. **Practice mindfulness**: Practice mindfulness by remaining present and attentive to the present moment.

By practicing these tips consistently, you can cultivate a more positive mindset and improve your mental health.

Chapter 4

Managing Stress and Anxiety

Managing Stress and Anxiety

Stress and anxiety are common experiences in our daily lives, and they can have a significant impact on our mental health and overall well-being. While some level of stress and anxiety is normal, when it becomes chronic or overwhelming, it can lead to serious mental and physical health problems.

In this chapter, we will explore the impact of stress and anxiety on our mental health and provide strategies for managing and reducing these experiences. We will discuss various techniques and practices, such as mindfulness, relaxation techniques, and self-care practices, that can help us manage stress and anxiety and improve our mental health. By learning to manage stress and anxiety, we can enhance our quality of life and achieve a greater sense of well-being.

The danger Stress and Anxiety pose to Mental Health

Stress and anxiety can have a significant impact on our mental health, affecting our thoughts, emotions, behaviors, and physical well-being. Chronic stress and anxiety can lead to a range of mental health problems, such as depression, panic disorder, and post-traumatic stress disorder (PTSD).

When we experience stress or anxiety, our body's natural stress response is activated, releasing hormones such as cortisol and adrenaline. This response can be helpful in short-term situations, such as when we need to escape danger, but when it becomes chronic, it can lead to a range of negative effects on our mental health.

Chronic stress and anxiety can cause us to feel overwhelmed, irritable, and fatigued. It can also lead to problems with sleep and appetite, and contribute to physical health problems such as heart disease and obesity. Additionally, it can cause negative changes in our thought patterns, such as increased negative self-talk and decreased self-esteem.

Recognizing the impact of stress and anxiety on our mental health is the first step towards managing these issues. By learning effective strategies for coping with stress and anxiety, we can improve our mental health and overall well-being.

Strategies for Managing Stress and Anxiety

There are many strategies that can be helpful in managing stress and anxiety. Here are a few examples:

- **Mindfulness and meditation**: These practices involve being present in the moment and focusing on your breath or a specific object. This can aid in relaxing your mind and alleviating feelings of stress and anxiety.

- **Exercise**: Physical activity can help to reduce stress and anxiety by releasing endorphins, which are feel-good chemicals in the brain. Engaging in physical activity can also enhance sleep quality, which is crucial for one's general mental well-being.

- **Relaxation techniques**: There are many techniques that can be used to promote relaxation, such as deep breathing, progressive muscle relaxation, and visualization. These techniques can help to reduce muscle tension and promote a sense of calm.

- **Self-care**: Self-care, which involves attending to your personal needs, is essential for effectively managing feelings of stress and anxiety. This can include activities such as getting enough sleep, eating a healthy diet, spending time with loved ones, and engaging in hobbies or other enjoyable activities.

- **Cognitive-behavioral therapy**: This type of therapy focuses on identifying and changing negative thought patterns that can contribute to stress and anxiety. A therapist can help you to develop coping strategies and tools to manage stress and anxiety.

It's important to note that not all strategies will work for everyone, and it may take some trial and error to find what works best for you. It's also important to seek professional help if you are struggling with chronic or severe stress and anxiety.

Chapter 5

Cultivating Resilience

Cultivating Resilience

Life is unpredictable, and we all face various challenges and obstacles throughout our lives. Some of these challenges can be difficult to cope with and may leave us feeling overwhelmed and defeated. However, the ability to bounce back from adversity and maintain a positive outlook is a trait known as resilience. Resilience is a crucial skill for maintaining good mental health and overall well-being.

In this chapter, we will explore the concept of resilience and how it can help us overcome adversity. We will also discuss the traits of resilient individuals and provide practical tips and exercises for cultivating resilience in ourselves. By developing our resilience, we can learn to face challenges with greater ease and emerge from difficult situations stronger and more resilient than ever before.

Exploring the concept of resilience and how it can help us bounce back from adversity

Resilience is the ability to adapt and cope with adversity, trauma, or significant stress in life. It is not about being invincible or never experiencing hardships, but rather about being able to bounce back from difficult situations. Resilience is not a fixed trait; it can be developed and strengthened over time with practice and effort.

When faced with adversity, resilient individuals are able to maintain a sense of control and perspective, and they can draw on their internal resources to cope effectively. They are often characterized by traits such as optimism, perseverance, self-awareness, and the ability to seek and accept support from others.

Research has shown that resilience is associated with a range of positive outcomes, including better mental health, higher life satisfaction, and greater well-being. It is a valuable tool for managing stress, anxiety, and other mental health challenges.

In order to cultivate resilience, it is important to develop a set of skills and strategies that can help you cope with adversity. These may include practicing self-care, building supportive relationships, developing problem-solving and decision-making skills, setting goals and taking action, and learning to adapt to change and uncertainty.

Through intentional practice and effort, anyone can develop and strengthen their resilience, leading to greater well-being and improved mental health outcomes.

Discussing the traits of resilient individuals

Resilience is the ability to recover from adversity, adapt to changes, and cope with stressors in a healthy way. Resilient individuals are often characterized by their ability to overcome setbacks and challenges, and to remain optimistic in the face of adversity.

Resilience is not something that people are born with; rather, it is a set of traits and behaviors that can be cultivated and developed over time. Some of the key traits of resilient individuals include:

- **Flexibility**: Resilient individuals are adaptable and able to adjust to new situations and challenges.

- **Optimism**: Resilient individuals tend to have a positive outlook on life and believe that they can overcome obstacles.

- **Proactivity**: Resilient individuals take action to address problems and challenges, rather than simply waiting for things to happen.

- **Emotional intelligence**: Resilient individuals are able to understand and manage their emotions effectively.

- **Social support**: Resilient individuals have strong relationships with friends and family, and are able to draw on these connections during times of stress and adversity.

By understanding these traits and behaviors, we can begin to develop our own resilience and build our capacity to overcome adversity.

How to develop these traits in ourselves

Developing resilience is an ongoing process that requires consistent effort and commitment. While some individuals may naturally possess some of the traits of resilience, it is possible for anyone to cultivate and strengthen these traits over time. Here are some tips for developing resilience:

1. **Practice self-care**: Prioritizing self-care can help you build the physical and emotional strength needed to handle challenges. This may involve obtaining sufficient sleep, consuming a nourishing diet, and participating in consistent physical activity.

2. **Build strong relationships**: Connecting with others and building a support network can help you feel more secure and less isolated during difficult times. Cultivate positive relationships with friends, family, and colleagues, and be sure to reach out for help when needed.

3. **Develop a growth mindset**: A growth mindset involves the belief that you can learn

and grow from challenges, setbacks, and failures. Focus on the lessons learned from past experiences, and approach new challenges with a willingness to learn and adapt.

4. **Set goals and take action**: Setting realistic goals and taking concrete steps towards achieving them can help you feel more empowered and in control. Divide bigger objectives into more feasible stages and acknowledge each accomplishment as you progress.

5. **Practice mindfulness**: Incorporate mindfulness into your routine, which entails being attentive to the current moment without passing judgment. Consistent mindfulness exercises can assist in cultivating heightened self-awareness and emotional control, both of which are crucial for fostering resilience.

By cultivating these habits and attitudes, you can develop the resilience needed to navigate life's challenges with greater ease and confidence.

Chapter 6
Building Strong Relationships

Chapter 6

Building Strong Relationships

Human beings are social creatures, and our relationships with others play a crucial role in our mental health and well-being. Positive social connections with friends, family, and romantic partners can provide us with emotional support, a sense of belonging, and increased feelings of happiness and life satisfaction. Conversely, a lack of social support or negative relationships can lead to feelings of isolation, loneliness, and poor mental health.

In this chapter, we will explore the importance of building strong relationships and maintaining healthy connections with others. We will discuss how positive relationships can benefit our mental health, as well as common pitfalls that can strain our relationships. Finally, we will provide practical tips for building and strengthening positive relationships with those around us.

In today's fast-paced and technology-driven world, many people struggle to find the time or energy to invest in their relationships. However, research has consistently shown that having a strong support network can significantly improve our mental health and well-being. By prioritizing our relationships and making an effort to connect with others, we can reap the benefits of positive social connections and build a foundation of resilience to help us cope with life's challenges.

Examining the impact of social support on mental health

Social support is an important factor that influences mental health. The relationships we have with others can impact our emotional well-being, and lack of social support can increase the risk of developing mental health problems. Studies have shown that individuals with strong social support networks are better equipped to deal with stress and are less likely to experience depression, anxiety, and other mental health disorders.

Social support can take many forms, including emotional, informational, and practical support. Emotional support refers to the comfort, care, and empathy that individuals provide to one another. Informational support includes the provision of advice and guidance, while practical support involves tangible assistance, such as help with tasks and errands.

Research has found that social support can be particularly important during times of stress and trauma. The presence of supportive individuals can buffer the negative effects of stress, reducing the risk of developing mental health problems. Additionally, social support can improve coping skills and increase feelings of self-worth and self-esteem.

However, it's important to note that social support is not a one-size-fits-all solution. The type and quality of social support needed can vary depending on the individual and the situation. What may be effective for one person might not work for another. For instance, some individuals might manage well with a few people in their support system, while others may need a broader network of supportive individuals. Social support is crucial for sustaining positive mental health.

By providing emotional, informational, and practical support, individuals can improve their ability to cope with stress and adversity. Strong relationships and social connections are crucial for overall well-being and can contribute to a more fulfilling and meaningful life.

Providing strategies for building and maintaining strong relationships, such as effective communication and boundary-setting

Establishing robust relationships is crucial for upholding good mental health. Whether it's with family, friends, or romantic partners, having a strong support system can make all the difference in times of stress or difficulty. However, building and maintaining strong relationships can be challenging. In this subtopic, we will explore some strategies for building and maintaining strong relationships.

Effective Communication: A vital element of any healthy relationship is effective communication. It's important to communicate clearly and openly with the people in our lives. This means being honest about our feelings and needs, and also being a good listener. When we communicate effectively, we can avoid misunderstandings and work together to resolve conflicts.

Active Listening: Active listening is a crucial skill for building strong relationships. It involves fully concentrating on what the other person is saying, rather than just waiting for our turn to speak. This means paying attention to both verbal and nonverbal cues, such as body language and tone of voice. Active listening shows the other person that we value and respect them, and can help to build trust and understanding.

Empathy: Empathy involves comprehending and sharing the emotions of another individual. It's an important aspect of building strong relationships because it helps us to connect with others on a deeper level. When we show empathy, we can validate the other person's feelings and provide them with the support they need.

Respect: Respect is a fundamental aspect of maintaining a healthy relationship. It means valuing the other person's feelings, needs, and boundaries. When we show respect, we can create a safe and supportive environment where both parties feel heard and understood.

Boundary-Setting: Boundaries are essential for maintaining healthy relationships. They allow us to communicate our needs and limits, and also help to prevent misunderstandings and conflicts. Setting boundaries can be challenging, but it's important to remember that they are necessary for building strong relationships.

Building and maintaining strong relationships is a crucial component of good mental health. By practicing effective communication, active listening, empathy, respect, and boundary-setting, we can create meaningful and fulfilling relationships with the people in our lives.

Chapter 7

Mindfulness and Self-Awareness

Mindfulness and Self-Awareness

In today's fast-paced world, it's easy to get caught up in the daily grind and forget to take a moment to breathe and reflect on our thoughts and feelings. Mindfulness and self-awareness are two powerful tools that can help us slow down, connect with ourselves, and improve our mental well-being.

Mindfulness involves being completely present in the current moment, without being distracted or critical. It involves paying attention to our thoughts, feelings, and physical sensations in a non-reactive way. Self-awareness, on the other hand, is the ability to recognize our own emotions, behaviors, and thought patterns.

Together, mindfulness and self-awareness can help us better understand ourselves and our experiences, cultivate greater compassion and empathy, and reduce stress and anxiety. In this chapter, we'll explore the benefits of mindfulness and self-awareness for mental health and provide practical tips and exercises for cultivating these skills in our daily lives.

Discussing the benefits of mindfulness and self-awareness for mental health

Mindfulness and self-awareness are practices that can have significant positive impacts on mental health. Mindfulness refers to the practice of being present and fully engaged in the current moment, without judgment. Self-awareness, on the other hand, involves understanding one's own thoughts, emotions, and behaviors, and how they affect oneself and others.

Research has shown that regular mindfulness practice can reduce symptoms of anxiety and depression, improve cognitive functioning, and increase resilience to stress. Mindfulness can also lead to greater self-awareness, allowing individuals to better understand their emotions and thought patterns, and to develop greater control over their responses to challenging situations.

Self-awareness, in turn, can help individuals identify and manage negative thoughts and emotions, and to make more intentional choices in their actions and behaviors. By understanding their own strengths and weaknesses, individuals can set more realistic goals and make more effective decisions in their personal and professional lives.

In summary, mindfulness and self-awareness are powerful tools for improving mental health and overall well-being. By practicing mindfulness and developing self-awareness, individuals can cultivate greater resilience, improve their relationships, and live more fulfilling lives.

Providing exercises and practices for cultivating mindfulness and self-awareness

Cultivating mindfulness and self-awareness can take time and practice, but the benefits for mental health are well worth the effort. Here are some exercises and practices to help you develop these skills:

- **Mindful Breathing**: Dedicate several minutes every day to concentrate on your breathing.. Sit in a comfortable position, close your eyes, and take deep breaths in through your nose and out through your mouth. Direct your attention to the feeling of the air flowing in and out of your body. Whenever your mind wanders, gently bring it back to your breath.

- **Body Scan**: Lie down or sit in a comfortable position and bring your attention to your body. Start at your feet and slowly scan your body, noticing any sensations, tension, or discomfort. Refrain from criticism or attempts to alter anything, simply observe. This can help you become more aware of physical sensations and release tension.

- **Gratitude Journaling**: Each day, write down three things you are grateful for. This can help you focus on the positive aspects of your life and shift your perspective.

- **Mindful Eating**: Pay attention to the taste, texture, and smell of your food as you eat it. Eat slowly and savor each bite. This can help you become more present and mindful in your daily life.

- **Self-Reflection**: Take some time each day to reflect on your thoughts and emotions. Ask yourself how you are feeling and why. This can help you become more aware of your inner experience and identify patterns or triggers.

Incorporating these practices into your daily routine, can help you develop greater mindfulness and self-awareness, which can help you better manage stress and improve your overall mental health.

Chapter 8

The Role of Physical Health

The Role of Physical Health

The well-established connection between mental and physical health is widely recognized. A healthy body leads to a healthy mind, and a healthy mind leads to a healthy body. When it comes to mental health, many people focus solely on psychological or emotional factors, neglecting the important role that physical health plays in overall well-being.

This chapter will delve into the correlation between physical health and mental health. We will discuss how physical health impacts mental health and vice versa. We will also provide practical strategies for improving physical health, which can in turn improve mental health outcomes.

The importance of physical health cannot be overstated. Maintaining good physical health helps to prevent chronic diseases, reduces the risk of mental health issues such as depression and anxiety, and improves cognitive functioning. Conversely, poor physical health can lead to an increased risk of mental health issues and can exacerbate existing mental health conditions.

Therefore, it is essential to prioritize physical health as part of a comprehensive approach to mental health. In the following sections, we will explore the ways in which physical health impacts mental health and provide strategies for improving physical health outcomes.

The relationship between physical health and mental health will be examined.

Physical health and mental health are intimately linked, with each influencing the other. Physical health refers to the state of the body, including its ability to function efficiently, while mental health refers to the state of the mind, including emotional and psychological well-being. When we talk about physical health, we often think of exercise, healthy eating habits, and regular check-ups with our doctors. However, physical health goes beyond these basic practices and also encompasses factors such as sleep, hydration, and stress management.

The connection between physical and mental health is evident in the way our bodies respond to stress. When we experience stress, whether it be from a difficult work assignment or a physical injury, our bodies release hormones such as cortisol and adrenaline in response. These hormones prepare our bodies for "fight or flight" mode, which can be useful in a short-term stressful situation. However, prolonged exposure to stress can cause these hormones to remain in our bodies, leading to chronic stress. Chronic stress can have a negative impact on our physical health by increasing the risk of conditions such as high blood pressure, heart disease, and diabetes. It can also lead to mental health issues such as anxiety and depression.

Conversely, taking care of our physical health can have a positive impact on our mental health. Exercise, for example, has been shown to release endorphins, the body's natural "feel-good" hormones. Regular exercise can also help reduce stress and anxiety and improve sleep quality, all of which can positively impact our mental health. In addition, a balanced and healthy diet can provide the body with the nutrients it needs to function optimally, which can improve our overall mood and energy levels.

Another important aspect of physical health is sleep. Adequate and restful sleep is essential for both our physical and mental well-being. Sleep allows our bodies to repair and restore themselves, which can reduce inflammation and improve immune function. Furthermore, it assists in regulating our emotions and mood, which can positively influence our mental health. On the other hand, lack of sleep or poor sleep quality can lead to increased stress, anxiety, and depression.

Hydration is also important for physical health. Our bodies are made up of mostly water, and dehydration can have a negative impact on our physical and mental well-being. Dehydration can cause fatigue, headaches, and even confusion, all of which can negatively impact our mental health.

It is evident that physical and mental health are intertwined. Taking care of our physical health through practices such as exercise, healthy eating, sleep, hydration, and stress management can have a positive impact on our mental health. On the other hand, neglecting our physical health can lead to negative impacts on our mental health. Therefore, it is essential to take a holistic approach to health and prioritize both physical and mental well-being.

Providing strategies for improving physical health, such as exercise and healthy eating, and discussing how these strategies can improve mental health as well

Maintaining good physical health is crucial for overall well-being, and research has shown that it is also closely linked to mental health. We will exploring strategies for improving physical health and how they can benefit mental health as well.

Regular exercise has numerous advantages for both physical and mental well-being, as studies have demonstrated. Exercise promotes cardiovascular health, strengthens the immune system, and reduces the risk of chronic ailments like diabetes and hypertension.. In addition, it can help to reduce symptoms of anxiety and depression, and improve mood and cognitive function. This is because exercise stimulates the release of endorphins, which are natural mood enhancers in the body.

Incorporating physical activity into your daily routine can be as simple as taking a walk, practicing yoga, or going for a swim. Even small amounts of physical activity can have a beneficial impact on physical and mental health.

Another important factor in physical health is nutrition. Eating a balanced diet that includes plenty of fruits, vegetables, lean proteins, and whole grains can help to reduce the risk of chronic diseases and improve overall physical health. In addition, certain foods have been shown to have specific benefits for mental health. For instance, research has linked omega-3 fatty acids found in fish and nuts to reduced symptoms of depression and anxiety.

Sufficient sleep is also critical for physical and mental health. Chronic sleep deprivation has been linked to an increased risk of obesity, diabetes, and cardiovascular disease, as well as anxiety and depression. Aim to get 7-8 hours of sleep per night and maintain a regular sleep schedule to regulate your body's internal clock.

Finally, reducing or eliminating detrimental substances such as alcohol and tobacco can significantly benefit both physical and mental health.

 Substance abuse has been linked to numerous health problems, including liver disease, cancer, and depression.

Making small changes to your daily routine, such as incorporating physical activity, eating a balanced diet, getting enough sleep, and avoiding harmful substances, can have a significant impact on both physical and mental health. By prioritizing physical health, you are also taking care of your mental health and overall well-being.

Dietary timetable that is essential for the development of our mental health

The connection between physical health and mental health cannot be overemphasized, and diet plays a crucial role in this connection. What we eat affects our mood, energy levels, and cognitive function. Therefore, it is essential to pay attention to our diet and ensure that we are consuming foods that promote mental health.

One crucial aspect of a healthy diet is having a proper dietary timetable. It is not only about the quality of the food but also about when and how often we eat. Our bodies have a natural rhythm that influences our eating habits, and it is essential to listen to our body's signals.

Breakfast is deemed as the most significant meal of the day. It provides the body with the necessary fuel and nutrients to start the day. A wholesome breakfast should consist of protein, whole grains, and beneficial fats. Examples of healthy breakfast options include oatmeal with nuts and berries, eggs with whole-grain toast, or a smoothie with fruits and vegetables.

Lunch should also include a balance of nutrients to provide energy for the rest of the day. It is essential to include vegetables, lean protein, and healthy carbohydrates. Examples of healthy lunch options include a salad with grilled chicken, whole-grain pasta with vegetables, or a wrap with hummus and vegetables.

Dinner should be a lighter meal and consumed a few hours before bedtime. It should include lean protein, vegetables, and healthy carbohydrates. Examples of healthy dinner options include grilled fish with roasted vegetables, brown rice with stir-fry vegetables, or a lentil soup with a side salad.

Snacks can also be incorporated into the dietary timetable, but they should be healthy and balanced. Snacks should include protein, healthy fats, and carbohydrates. Examples of healthy snacks include a piece of fruit with nut butter, vegetables with hummus, or a small serving of Greek yogurt with berries.

Having a proper dietary timetable is essential for the development of our mental health. It is important to include a balance of nutrients in our meals and listen to our body's signals. By incorporating healthy food choices into our daily routine, we can improve our mental health and overall well-being.

Chapter 9
Overcoming Mental Health Challenges

Overcoming Mental Health Challenges

Mental health challenges can be a difficult and often isolating experience for many individuals. Coping with symptoms such as depression, anxiety, or trauma can be overwhelming and impact various aspects of daily life. However, it is important to recognize that these challenges are treatable, and with the right support, individuals can overcome them and lead fulfilling lives.

In this chapter, we will explore different approaches and strategies for overcoming mental health challenges. We will discuss the importance of seeking professional help, as well as incorporating self-care practices and utilizing social support systems. We will also examine how resilience and a growth mindset can play a role in overcoming challenges and building mental strength.

By understanding these various approaches and strategies, individuals can develop a personalized plan for overcoming their specific mental health challenges and ultimately improve their quality of life.

Discussing common mental health challenges, such as depression and anxiety, and how to overcome them

Mental health challenges can affect anyone, regardless of age, gender, or background. Common mental health challenges include depression, anxiety, bipolar disorder, post-traumatic stress disorder (PTSD), and schizophrenia. While each of these conditions presents unique challenges, they can all be overcome with the right strategies and support.

Depression, for example, is a mood disorder that can cause feelings of sadness, hopelessness, and a lack of interest in activities once enjoyed. One effective way to overcome depression is through therapy, such as cognitive-behavioral therapy (CBT), which helps individuals identify and change negative thought patterns. Antidepressant medication can also be helpful in treating depression, but should always be used under the guidance of a healthcare professional.

Anxiety, on the other hand, is characterized by excessive worry and fear about everyday situations. It can manifest in a variety of ways, including panic attacks, obsessive-compulsive behaviors, and phobias. To overcome anxiety, individuals can benefit from learning relaxation techniques such as deep breathing and progressive muscle relaxation, and practicing mindfulness meditation. CBT can also be an effective treatment for anxiety by helping individuals to identify and challenge irrational thoughts.

Bipolar disorder is a mood disorder that causes extreme fluctuations in mood, energy levels, and activity levels. To overcome bipolar disorder, medication and therapy are often used in combination. Medications such as mood stabilizers and antipsychotics can help manage symptoms, while therapy can help individuals learn coping strategies and build a support system.

PTSD is a mental health condition that can develop after a traumatic event, such as experiencing or witnessing violence, combat, or sexual assault. Treatment for PTSD often involves therapy, such as cognitive processing therapy (CPT) and eye movement desensitization and reprocessing (EMDR), which help individuals process and reframe traumatic memories.

Schizophrenia is a persistent mental health disorder that impedes an individual's capacity to think, feel, and behave lucidly. Treatment for schizophrenia often involves a combination of medication and therapy, such as cognitive remediation therapy and social skills training, which can help individuals manage symptoms and improve their ability to function in daily life.

In addition to these conditions, there are many other mental health challenges that individuals may face. It is important to seek professional help and support from loved ones when dealing with mental health challenges, as recovery is often a journey that requires a combination of medical and psychological interventions.

It is also important to remember that recovery is possible, and that many individuals with mental health challenges go on to live full and meaningful lives. By taking care of oneself through proper treatment, self-care, and support, it is possible to overcome mental health challenges and achieve a sense of well-being and happiness.

Providing resources and support for readers who are struggling with mental health issues

Accessing resources and support is crucial for individuals who are struggling with mental health challenges. Fortunately, there are various resources and support systems available to those who need them. In this subtopic, we will discuss some of the resources and support systems that individuals can utilize to overcome their mental health challenges.

1. **Therapy and Counseling**: Therapy and counseling are effective treatments for individuals struggling with mental health issues. Therapists and counselors provide a safe and non-judgmental space for

individuals to express their thoughts and feelings. They also offer practical tools and strategies to help individuals manage their symptoms and improve their overall mental health. There are different types of therapy, including cognitive-behavioral therapy, dialectical behavior therapy, and psychodynamic therapy, among others. It is important to find a therapist who specializes in treating the specific mental health condition that one is dealing with.

2. **Support Groups**: Support groups are a great resource for individuals who are struggling with mental health challenges. These groups bring together individuals who share similar experiences, allowing them to connect with others who understand what they are going through. Support groups can be found both in-person and online, and they provide a supportive and understanding environment where individuals can share their experiences, offer each other support and advice, and learn from each other.

3. **Crisis Hotlines**: Crisis hotlines are available 24/7 and offer immediate support for individuals who are in crisis. These hotlines provide confidential support and can help individuals cope with overwhelming emotions, suicidal thoughts, and other mental health issues. The National Suicide Prevention Lifeline (1-800-273-TALK) is one example of a crisis hotline that provides support and resources to individuals who are struggling with mental health challenges.

4. **Self-Help Resources**: There are many self-help resources available to individuals who are struggling with mental health challenges. These resources include books, podcasts, online forums, and apps, among others. These resources provide practical tools and strategies that individuals can use to manage their symptoms and improve their mental health. It is important to note that while self-help resources can be useful, they should not be used as a substitute for professional treatment.

5. **Medication**: In some cases, medication may be necessary to treat mental health issues. Medication can help individuals manage their symptoms and improve their mental health. However, medication should always be prescribed and monitored by a healthcare professional. It is important to discuss the potential risks and benefits of medication with a healthcare provider before starting any medication.

In conclusion, there are various resources and support systems available to individuals who are struggling with mental health challenges. These resources include therapy and counseling, support groups, crisis hotlines, self-help resources, and medication. It is important for individuals to access the resources and support that they need to overcome their mental health challenges. By utilizing these resources, individuals can improve their mental health and overall quality of life.

Chapter 10

Maintaining a Healthy Mind Space

Maintaining a Healthy Mind Space

In the previous chapters, we have discussed various ways to improve our mental health and wellbeing. However, maintaining a healthy mind space is an ongoing process that requires continuous effort and attention. Chapter 10 will focus on practical tips and strategies for maintaining a healthy mind space and incorporating these practices into our daily lives.

The importance of maintaining a healthy mind space cannot be overstated. Our mental health affects every aspect of our lives, from our relationships and work to our physical health and overall happiness. By taking care of our mental health, we can improve our quality of life and achieve greater success in all areas.

In this chapter, we will explore the importance of self-care, stress management, and finding balance in our lives. We will also discuss how to build resilience and maintain a positive mindset, even in challenging times. By following these tips and strategies, we can cultivate a healthy mind space and thrive in all areas of our lives.

The importance of self-care, stress management, and finding balance in our lives

Self-care, stress management, and finding balance are essential components of maintaining a healthy mind space. Taking care of ourselves physically, emotionally, and mentally can help us to feel more positive, reduce stress, and prevent burnout. Here are some ways to implement these practices:

- **Self-Care**: Self-care is any activity that we do deliberately to take care of ourselves physically, emotionally, and mentally. It can range from simple acts like taking a walk, reading a book, or taking a warm bath, to more intentional practices like meditation, yoga, or therapy. Self-care helps us to reduce stress, improve our mood, and increase our overall sense of well-being.

- **Stress Management**: Stress is a normal part of life, but it can become overwhelming if we don't manage it properly. Stress management techniques include exercise, deep breathing, mindfulness, and time management. These practices can help us to feel more in control and reduce the negative effects of stress on our bodies and minds.

- **Finding Balance**: Finding balance in our lives means prioritizing the things that are most important to us and making time for them. This might include spending time with loved ones, pursuing hobbies or interests, or simply taking time for ourselves. By finding balance, we can reduce stress, improve our relationships, and increase our overall happiness.

It's important to note that self-care, stress management, and finding balance are ongoing practices that require consistent effort. It's not enough to do them once in a while and expect to see lasting results. Instead, we must make them a regular part of our daily routine in order to reap the full benefits.

In addition to these practices, it's important to seek support from others when needed. This might include talking to a trusted friend or family member, joining a support group, or seeking professional help from a therapist or counselor.

By prioritizing self-care, stress management, and finding balance in our lives, we can maintain a healthy mind space and improve our overall well-being.

Providing practical tips for maintaining a healthy mind space over the long term

Maintaining a healthy mind space is a lifelong process that requires continuous effort and commitment. Here are some practical tips for cultivating a healthy mind space over the long term:

1. **Practice self-care regularly**: Self-care is essential for maintaining a healthy mind space. Engage in activities that you enjoy and that help you to relax and recharge. This

can include things like taking a warm bath, reading a good book, practicing yoga or meditation, or spending time outdoors in nature.

2. **Practice stress-management techniques**: Stress can have a significant impact on our mental health. As a result, it is crucial to establish practical methods for managing stress. This can include things like deep breathing exercises, progressive muscle relaxation, or guided imagery.

3. **Practice healthy habits**: Maintaining healthy habits can help to improve our overall well-being. This includes things like getting enough sleep, eating a healthy diet, and engaging in regular exercise.

4. **Cultivate positive relationships**: Strong social connections are essential for maintaining a healthy mind space. Take the time to nurture your relationships with family and friends, and consider joining a community group or organization where you can meet new people.

5. **Set realistic goals**: Setting realistic goals can help to provide a sense of purpose and motivation, which can be beneficial for our mental health. However, it is important to ensure that these goals are achievable and that we do not become overwhelmed or stressed trying to achieve them.

6. **Practice mindfulness and gratitude**: Practicing mindfulness and gratitude can help to promote a positive mindset and improve our overall well-being. Take the time to appreciate the good things in your life, and practice mindfulness techniques like deep breathing and body scanning.

7. **Seek support when needed**: Finally, it is important to seek support when needed. This can include talking to a trusted friend or family member, seeking professional counseling or therapy, or joining a support group for individuals struggling with mental health issues.

In conclusion, maintaining a healthy mind space is an ongoing process that requires dedication and effort. By practicing self-care, stress-management techniques, healthy habits, cultivating positive relationships, setting realistic goals, practicing mindfulness and gratitude, and seeking support when needed, we can improve our mental health and well-being over the long term.

Summarizing the key takeaways from the book

Throughout this book, we have explored various strategies for improving our mental health and maintaining a healthy mind space. Some of the significant points to remember from this book are:

1. Self-awareness is essential for maintaining good mental health. We must be aware of our thoughts, emotions, and behaviors in order to identify areas that need improvement.

2. Building and maintaining strong relationships is crucial for our mental health. We need social support to help us through difficult times.

3. Mindfulness and meditation can help us cultivate a sense of inner peace and reduce stress and anxiety.

4. Regular exercise and healthy eating habits are not only important for our physical health, but also for our mental health.

5. We must learn to manage stress and anxiety, and develop resilience to overcome adversity.

6. Seeking professional help when necessary is important for our mental health. There is no shame in asking for help.

7. Finally, taking care of ourselves and prioritizing self-care is crucial for maintaining a healthy mind space over the long term.

By implementing these strategies, we can cultivate a healthier mind space and improve our overall well-being. It is important to remember that mental health is just as important as physical health and should be prioritized and taken care of regularly.

www.ingramcontent.com/pod-product-compliance
Lightning Source LLC
Chambersburg PA
CBHW070740250726
48662CB00004B/1596